Celebrating Lunar New Year

Katie Peters

GRL Consultant Diane Craig,
Certified Literacy Specialist

Lerner Publications ◆ Minneapolis

Note from a GRL Consultant
This Pull Ahead leveled book has been carefully designed for beginning readers. A team of guided reading literacy experts has reviewed and leveled the book to ensure readers pull ahead and experience success.

Lerner Publications
An imprint of Lerner Publishing Group, Inc.
241 First Avenue North
Minneapolis, MN 55401 USA

For reading levels and more information, look up this title at www.lernerbooks.com.

Main body text set in Memphis Pro 24/39
Typeface provided by Linotype.

Photo Acknowledgments
The images in this book are used with the permission of: © phive/Shutterstock Images, p. 3; © Steve Edreff/Shutterstock Images, pp. 4–5; © Dragon Images/Shutterstock Images, pp. 6–7, 16 (left); © Captain Wang/Shutterstock Images, pp. 8–9, 16 (middle); © FamVeld/Shutterstock Images, pp. 10–11, 14–15; © Tuleyhcm/Shutterstock Images, pp. 12–13, 16 (right).

Front Cover: © Inspiration GP/Shutterstock Images

Library of Congress Cataloging-in-Publication Data

Names: Peters, Katie, author.
Title: Celebrating Lunar New Year / Katie Peters.
Description: Minneapolis, MN : Lerner Publications, [2026] | Series: Let's celebrate holidays (Pull Ahead Readers – nonfiction) | Includes index. | Audience: Ages 4–7 | Audience: Grades K–1 | Summary: "Red lanterns, red envelopes, red everything; during Lunar New Year the color red is lucky. Vibrant photographs and easy-to-read text help young readers celebrate this holiday. Pairs with the story, David's Lunar New Year Celebrations"—Provided by publisher.
Identifiers: LCCN 2024038593 (print) | LCCN 2024038594 (ebook) | ISBN 9798765668740 (library binding) | ISBN 9798765684412 (paperback) | ISBN 9798765678695 (epub)
Subjects: LCSH: Chinese New Year—Juvenile literature.
Classification: LCC GT4905 .P4622 2026 (print) | LCC GT4905 (ebook) | DDC 394.261—dc23/eng/20240826

LC record available at https://lccn.loc.gov/2024038593
LC ebook record available at https://lccn.loc.gov/2024038594

Manufactured in the United States of America
1 – CG – 7/15/25

Table of Contents

Celebrating Lunar New Year

Lunar New Year is in the first two months of the year.

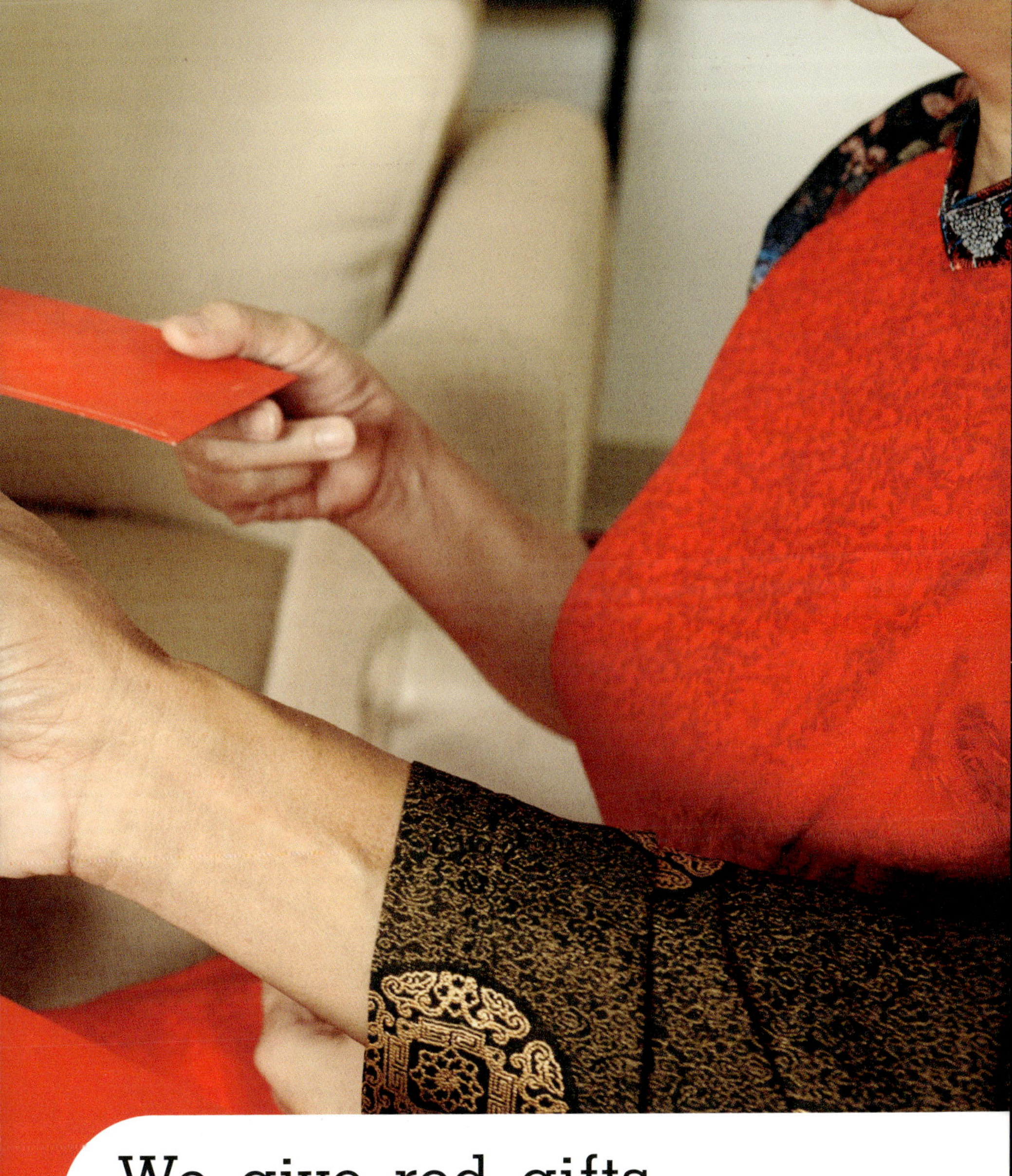

We give red gifts.
Red is a lucky color.

We hang red lamps.

We eat a special dinner.

We go to a parade.

We wish one another good luck for the new year!

Did You See It?

gifts

lamp

parade

Index